Master the 12 Universal Laws

A Guide to Manifestation, Energy Healing, Spiritual Growth and Mindfulness

Jamie Morgan

Contents

Chapter One

Introduction

In the vast expanse of existence, where time, space, and consciousness converge, there exist fundamental principles—universal laws—that underpin the very essence of our reality. These immutable laws act as the guiding forces of the cosmos, influencing the motion of celestial bodies, the course of natural phenomena, and the rhythm of human experiences. They are the invisible architects of our universe, molding the way we interact with the world around us and shaping our individual and collective journeys.

Among these core principles are the 12 universal laws, a series of cosmic truths that, when understood and embraced, can lead us toward a life marked by depth, harmony, and greater fulfillment. Each law, unique in its nature, yet interconnected with the rest, shines a light on the path to navigating life's complexities with insight and equilibrium. Engaging with these laws is more than an intellectual endeavor—it is an invitation to a profound personal transformation, a call to align our inner essence with the vastness of the universe outside.

The significance of these laws extends beyond theoretical speculation; they are practical instruments for changing our lives and the world around us. By integrating the wisdom of these laws into our everyday existence, we unlock the door to crafting a reality that mirrors our noblest dreams and truest selves. This process of alignment is an adventure in self-discovery, urging us to look beyond the tangible, to resonate with the subtle energies of existence, and to realize the immense power we possess to direct our life's course.

As we dive into this exploration, let's do so with open hearts and curious minds, eager to absorb the ancient knowledge and to find the beautiful balance that emerges when we live in harmony with the grand principles that orchestrate all of creation. Understanding and applying the 12 universal laws opens up a realm of possibility, guiding us to a more expansive, balanced, and enriching life, unveiling the boundless potential that dwells within each of us.

Chapter Two

The Law of Polarity

The Law of Polarity presents us with a universe of dualities: a world where light cannot exist without darkness, silence is defined by the presence of sound, and joy is only truly grasped when acquainted with sorrow. This law posits that everything is on a continuum and has an opposite. We can understand and experience life fully only through the contrasts it offers.

Consider the Law of Polarity as the great harmonizer, the force that unites the yin and yang within the vast expanse of existence. It is the law that teaches us that when we find ourselves in the depths of despair, we are merely a breath away from hope. When we encounter difficulty, we are simultaneously presented with an opportunity. This law is significant because it is a reminder that life is a balancing act, constantly moving and seeking equilibrium.

In the grand universe, every experience serves a purpose. The Law of Polarity ensures a world rich with color and texture, giving depth to our human experience. It invites us to shift our perspective, to see the hidden treasures in our struggles, and to appreciate the full spectrum of human emotion and experience.

By embracing this law, we gain a more profound appreciation for the contrasts that fill our world. We start to see that the existence of something is defined by the existence of its opposite. Wealth has meaning because of poverty, health gains its value through sickness, and love is often most deeply felt in the face of loss. This understanding can lead us to a more centered and balanced life, where we see obstacles as gateways to personal evolution and growth.

In real-life, the Law of Polarity can be seen in numerous scenarios that reflect the dichotomy of our existence. Take, for instance, the story of a young entrepreneur whose first business venture failed miserably. Where many might see failure, the Law of Polarity suggests a different perspective — an opportunity for learning and growth. From the ashes of this failed enterprise, the entrepreneur learned invaluable lessons that became the foundation of a future successful business. The initial loss and subsequent victory are two poles on the same spectrum, illustrating how polar opposites provide a complete understanding of an experience.

Consider also the journey of an artist who finds true creative expression only after grappling with periods of intense block and frustration. The struggle is as integral to the creative process as the moments of flow and inspiration. The Law of Polarity is at play here, teaching that the frustration fuels the eventual breakthrough, and the presence of one state defines the other.

Or, reflect upon the individual who overcomes a health challenge only to emerge with a stronger appreciation for life and wellness. Their sickness is not an isolated misfortune but a point on the spectrum that intensifies their experience of health once it is regained. This contrast between illness and health brings a profound understanding and gratitude for the latter, which may not have been as potent without the experience of the former.

Moreover, consider the collective human experience during times of crisis, such as natural disasters. Communities often experience a surge in unity and altruism in the aftermath of adversity. The polarity of isolation and despair juxtaposed with unity and hope demonstrates how the best of human qualities often shine brightest against the backdrop of hardship.

These examples serve to illustrate the Law of Polarity in action — a universal principle reminding us that our darkest moments may lead to the brightest outcomes and that within every adverse situation lies the potential for a beneficial counterpart. As we move forward, we'll discover how to consciously apply this law, finding balance and harmony in the polarities that define our lives.

As we delve into the practical applications of the Law of Polarity, consider these exercises designed to help you identify and appreciate the polarities in your own life:

Exercise 1: The Polarity Reflection Journal

Keep a journal for a week. Each day, write down an event or situation you experienced that elicited a strong emotional response, whether positive or negative. Next to this, write down the opposite potential within that situation. For example, if you felt disappointment over a missed opportunity, identify the potential space it created for something new to enter your life.

Exercise 2: The Opposite Side Meditation

Sit quietly and think of a current challenge in your life. Close your eyes and visualize this challenge. Now, mentally explore the opposite of this challenge. What does it look like? How does it feel? Spend a few minutes each day trying to embody the feeling of the opposite, positive polarity of your challenge.

Exercise 3: The Polarity Swap

Choose a day to practice the 'polarity swap.' Whenever you encounter a negative thought, consciously replace it with its positive opposite. For instance, if you catch yourself thinking, "I'm not good at this," immediately swap it for, "I am continually improving at this." Notice how this shift in perspective affects your mood and actions throughout the day.

Exercise 4: The Gratitude Flip

Write down three things you're struggling with or are a source of stress. Next to each, write down at least one reason you can be grateful for that challenge. What has it taught you? How has it made you stronger or wiser? This exercise helps to reframe challenges as opportunities for gratitude.

Exercise 5: The Role Reversal

Think of a person with whom you have a challenging relationship. Write down traits or actions of theirs that frustrate you. Now, write down how these traits might be beneficial or necessary in certain situations or how they might stem from that person's own challenges. This helps to see the positive aspects or intentions behind behaviors, cultivating empathy and understanding.

Exercise 6: The Balance Scale

Visualize a balance scale. On one side, place a recent event that you consider negative. On the opposite side, try to balance it with a positive aspect of your life. This visualization helps you to see your life in a broader perspective and understand that positives and negatives often coexist and balance each other out.

By regularly engaging with these exercises, you can begin to see the Law of Polarity at work in your life. This awareness can transform your perception, enabling you to find a hidden strength in adversity and a humble perspective in triumph. Through this practice, you will cultivate a sense of balance that honors the full range of human experience.

Chapter Three

The Law of Action

The Law of Action serves as the bridge between possibility and reality. This law underscores a fundamental truth: while intention plants the seeds of our future, it is action that waters these seeds, nurturing them into fruition. The importance of action over mere intention cannot be overstated; it is the force that propels us forward, turning the invisible into the visible, the imagined into the tangible.

The Law of Action operates on the principle that our intentions, thoughts, and feelings must be matched with concrete steps towards our goals. It's a call to arms, urging us not to remain passive spectators in our lives but to become active participants in crafting our destiny. This law reminds us that the universe itself is in constant motion, and by aligning our actions with our deepest desires, we move in harmony with the cosmos, co-creating our reality with the energy that animates all of existence.

Consider the dreamer who envisions a masterpiece but never picks up the brush, the wanderer who dreams of distant lands but never takes a step outside their door, or the aspiring author who carries a novel in their heart but never sets pen to paper. In each case, the potential for greatness exists, but without action, these dreams remain just out of reach, specters of what could be.

The Law of Action teaches us that intention alone is like a boat without sails; it may have the potential to journey across vast oceans, but without action, it remains moored to the shore. Action is the wind that fills the sails, propelling the boat forward on its journey. It's important to recognize that action doesn't always necessitate grand gestures or monumental steps; even the smallest actions can set the wheels of change in motion, creating ripples that expand across the pond of our existence.

Furthermore, this law illuminates the truth that procrastination and fear are the antithesis of action. Procrastination delays our progress, and fear can paralyze us, keeping us from taking the steps necessary to achieve our dreams. By understanding and applying the Law of Action, we learn to navigate through these barriers, stepping boldly towards our goals with determination and courage.

In embracing the Law of Action, we also come to understand the importance of timing and discernment. Not all actions are created equal, and mindless activity can be as counterproductive as inaction. Therefore, the Law of Action encourages us to act not only with intention but with awareness and wisdom, ensuring that our actions are aligned with our highest good and the natural flow of the universe.

To harness the power of the Law of Action and move toward achieving your goals, consider integrating these actionable steps into your daily life. These suggestions are designed to transform intention into action, helping you to navigate the journey from where you are now to where you wish to be.

1. Break Your Goal into Manageable Steps

Begin by breaking down your larger goal into smaller, more manageable tasks. Each task should be clear and specific enough to act upon. This approach reduces overwhelm and creates a clear path forward, making your goal feel more attainable.

2. Set Daily Intentions

Each morning, set a daily intention that aligns with your larger goal. This could be as simple as dedicating 15 minutes to research, reaching out to a potential mentor, or writing a page of your book. Daily intentions keep your goal at the forefront of your mind and ensure consistent progress.

3. Create a Timeline

Establish a realistic timeline for your goal with specific milestones. Deadlines create a sense of urgency that can motivate action. Be sure to celebrate small victories along the way to maintain motivation.

4. Implement a Daily Habit Related to Your Goal

Identify one small habit that can contribute to your goal and integrate it into your daily routine. Whether it's practicing a new language for ten minutes a day, meditating to improve focus, or jotting down ideas, consistent action builds momentum.

5. Use Visual Reminders

Place visual reminders of your goal in your environment. This could be a vision board, a goal-related quote on your mirror, or a picture of your dream destination. Visual cues can inspire action and keep your goal top of mind.

6. Seek Accountability

Share your goal with a trusted friend, family member, or mentor who can offer support and hold you accountable. Regular check-ins can provide motivation and encourage you to stay on track.

7. Reflect and Adjust

Regularly reflect on your progress and be willing to adjust your approach as needed. Flexibility is key; if a particular strategy isn't working, be open to trying something new. Reflection also allows you to recognize and overcome any patterns of procrastination or resistance.

8. Embrace Learning Opportunities

View each step towards your goal as an opportunity to learn and grow. This mindset can transform challenges into valuable experiences, making the journey as rewarding as the destination.

9. Prioritize Self-Care

Ensure that your action plan includes self-care practices. Maintaining your physical, mental, and emotional well-being can enhance your energy and focus, making it easier to take consistent action towards your goal.

10. Celebrate Progress

Acknowledge and celebrate your progress, no matter how small. Celebrating milestones reinforces positive behavior and keeps you motivated to continue.

To deepen your understanding and application of the Law of Action, consider engaging with the following reflection prompts. These questions are designed to inspire introspection and active engagement with the law, encouraging you to transform thought into purposeful action.

1. Clarify Your Vision

- What specific goal or dream am I working towards?

- Why is this goal important to me, and how does it align with my values and aspirations?

2. Assess Your Actions

- In what ways have I already taken action towards my goal?

- Are there actions I've been avoiding or postponing? If so, what has been holding me back?

3. Overcome Barriers

- What are the primary obstacles or fears that prevent me from taking action?

- How can I address these barriers in small, manageable steps?

4. Leverage Resources

- What resources (people, tools, information) do I currently have at my disposal that can assist me in taking action?

- Are there additional resources I need to seek out?

5. Implement Daily Habits

- What daily habit can I introduce into my routine that will consistently move me closer to my goal?

- How will I ensure that I stick to this habit?

6. Prioritize Tasks

- Which actions will have the most significant impact on achieving my goal?

- How can I prioritize these actions to ensure they receive my focus and energy?

7. Reflect on Progress

- How will I measure my progress towards my goal?

- What milestones can I celebrate along the way to keep myself motivated?

8. Adapt and Adjust

- Am I willing to adjust my plan if I encounter unexpected challenges or if certain strategies are not working?

- How can I remain flexible and open to new approaches while staying committed to my goal?

9. Seek Support

- Who in my life can offer support, guidance, or accountability as I work towards my goal?

- How can I engage with these individuals to enhance my journey?

10. Embrace the Journey

- How can I ensure that I enjoy the process and not just focus on the end goal?

- What lessons am I learning along the way, and how am I growing as a person?

By regularly reflecting on these prompts, you engage in an active dialogue with yourself about your goals, the actions required to achieve them, and the obstacles that may arise. This reflective practice not only reinforces your commitment to the Law of Action but also deepens your understanding of its role in your personal growth and achievement.

Chapter Four

The Law of Vibration

The Law of Vibration, invites us to see the world not as a collection of static entities, but as a dynamic dance of energy. From the vastness of space to the minute particles that constitute the essence of all matter, vibration is the universal language of existence.

This law teaches us that the seemingly solid world is, at its core, a symphony of energetic frequencies. Each atom, each thought, and each emotion emits its own unique vibration, contributing to the infinite chorus that composes the universe. It's a concept that bridges the gap between the tangible and the intangible, offering a glimpse into the interconnectedness of all things.

Understanding that vibration underlies the fabric of reality revolutionizes our perception of life. It becomes clear that our thoughts and emotions are not merely ephemeral but are powerful vibrational forces capable of influencing the material world. Positive thoughts and emotions vibrate at higher frequencies, radiating outward and attracting circumstances and experiences of a similar vibrational nature. Conversely, negative thoughts lower our vibrational frequency, potentially leading to less desirable outcomes.

The beauty of this law lies in its empowerment. Recognizing that we are vibrational beings gives us the power to consciously tune our energetic frequency. Like tuning an instrument to the desired pitch, we can adjust our thoughts, emotions, and actions to resonate with the frequencies of love, joy, and abundance. This is not merely a passive acknowledgment but an active engagement with the energetic universe, a deliberate choice to align ourselves with the vibrations that uplift and inspire.

Navigating the currents of our vibrational existence offers a powerful pathway to transformation. By consciously elevating our vibrational frequency, we align more closely with the energies of abundance, joy, and peace. Here are practical tips for harnessing the power of your thoughts, emotions, and actions to raise your vibrational state:

1. Cultivate Positive Thoughts: Thoughts are the seeds of our reality. Cultivating a garden of positive thoughts can significantly elevate your vibrational frequency. Begin each day by setting an intention for positivity and gratitude. When negative thoughts surface, acknowledge them, then gently redirect your focus to thoughts that uplift and inspire.

2. Embrace Emotional Awareness: Emotions are powerful indicators of our vibrational state. By becoming more aware of your emotions, you can choose responses that elevate rather than diminish your energy. Practice observing your emotions without judgment, allowing yourself to feel and then consciously choosing to shift towards more positive emotional states.

3. Practice Mindfulness and Meditation: Mindfulness and meditation are invaluable tools for tuning into the present moment and calming the mind. Regular practice can help clear mental clutter, reducing stress and anxiety, and thereby raising your vibrational frequency. Even a few minutes a day can have profound effects on your overall well-being.

4. Engage in Acts of Kindness: Acts of kindness and generosity emit high vibrations, benefiting both the giver and the receiver. Look for opportunities to help others, whether through volunteering, offering support to a friend, or simply sharing a smile with a stranger. These actions create ripples of positive energy that elevate your vibration and those around you.

5. Connect with Nature: Nature vibrates at a frequency of harmony and balance. Spending time outdoors, whether walking in a park, gardening, or simply sitting under a tree, can help align your energy with the natural world, promoting a sense of peace and well-being.

6. Nourish Your Body: The food we eat and the way we treat our bodies have a significant impact on our vibrational frequency. Opt for foods that are alive and vibrant, filled with the energy of the sun. Exercise regularly to move energy through your body, and ensure you get enough rest to recharge your vibrational state.

7. Surround Yourself with Positive Influences: The environment and company you keep can influence your vibrational frequency. Surround yourself with positive people who uplift and support you. Create a living and working space that reflects beauty and inspiration, filling it with objects, colors, and sounds that resonate with your higher vibrational state.

8. Practice Forgiveness and Letting Go: Holding onto grievances, anger, or regret can significantly lower your vibration. Practice forgiveness, not just towards others but towards yourself. Letting go of past hurts frees you from negative energetic ties, allowing your vibration to rise.

9. Express Yourself Creatively: Creativity is a high-vibrational activity. Engage in creative pursuits that bring you joy, whether painting, writing, dancing, or cooking. Creative expression is a powerful way to channel and elevate your energy.

10. Be True to Yourself: Honoring your authentic self is perhaps the most powerful way to raise your vibration. Listen to your inner voice, follow your passions, and align your life with your true essence. Authenticity resonates with a high frequency, attracting experiences and relationships that reflect your genuine self.

To truly embrace the Law of Vibration and harness its transformative power, engaging in activities that allow you to consciously tune into and alter your vibrational state can be profoundly impactful. Here are some practical activities designed to help you become more attuned to your own energy and actively work towards elevating it:

1. Vibrational Journaling:

Keep a daily journal where you note your vibrational state at different times. Record what activities, thoughts, or interactions led to changes in your vibration. Over time, this practice can help you identify patterns and triggers, empowering you to cultivate more of what enhances your vibration and reduce what lowers it.

2. Gratitude Practice:

Start or end your day by listing three things you're grateful for. Gratitude naturally elevates your vibration by shifting your focus from lack to abundance. The more you practice gratitude, the more you'll notice an uplift in your overall energetic state.

3. Energy Cleansing Rituals:

Incorporate simple cleansing rituals into your routine, such as sage smudging your living space, taking salt baths, or visualizing a white light enveloping and purifying your energy field. These practices can help clear away lower vibrations and create space for higher frequencies.

4. High-Vibe Music and Sounds:

Music and sounds have a direct impact on our vibrational state. Create a playlist of songs or sounds that uplift you. Instruments like singing bowls, bells, and tuning forks are especially known for their vibrational healing properties.

5. Movement and Dance:

Physical movement is a powerful way to shift energy and raise your vibration. Engage in activities that you enjoy, such as yoga, dancing, walking in nature, or any form of exercise that makes you feel alive and vibrant.

6. Positive Affirmations:

Craft a set of personal affirmations that resonate with the high-vibrational life you wish to lead. Recite these affirmations daily, especially in the morning or before bed, to reprogram your subconscious and align your energy with your intentions.

7. Mindful Breathing:

Practice mindful breathing exercises to center yourself and connect with your current vibrational state. Deep, conscious breathing can help calm the mind, release stress, and elevate your energy.

8. Visualization Exercises:

Spend time visualizing your ideal vibrational state. Imagine yourself surrounded by a radiant light that represents the highest frequency.

Feel this light infusing every cell of your body, lifting your energy and aligning you with your highest potential.

9. Connect with High-Vibrational Environments:

Spend time in environments that naturally have a high vibration, such as near the ocean, in a forest, or a place filled with art and beauty. Nature, in particular, has a harmonizing effect on our energy and can help raise our vibrational frequency.

10. Acts of Kindness and Service:

Engaging in acts of kindness and service naturally elevates your vibration and the vibration of those around you. Look for opportunities to help others in your community or contribute to causes you care about. The joy and fulfillment derived from service are powerful vibration boosters.

By incorporating these activities into your life, you actively participate in shaping your vibrational reality. Remember, tuning into and altering your vibration is a practice—a journey of becoming more consciously aware of the energy you carry and the energy you wish to embody. As you explore these activities, remain open and curious about the shifts you experience, trusting in your innate ability to navigate the beautiful vibrational landscape of your life.

Chapter Five

The Law of Cause and Effect

This universal law eloquently illustrates the interconnectedness of actions and outcomes, teaching us that every action we take has a corresponding reaction, a ripple that extends far beyond the initial splash. It is the cosmic ledger, ensuring that nothing in this universe operates in isolation; every thought, word, and deed is a cause that sets in motion a chain of effects, weaving the fabric of our reality.

The Law of Cause and Effect serves as a profound reminder of our power and responsibility. It compels us to look closely at the seeds we sow with our choices, for the harvest we reap tomorrow is born from the seeds we plant today. This law does not punish nor reward; it simply is—a neutral, unbiased force that responds to our energetic contributions to the world.

Understanding this law invites us to become more mindful architects of our lives. It encourages us to pause and consider the potential effects of our actions, not just on ourselves, but on the world around us. By aligning our actions with positive intentions and higher principles, we set into motion a series of effects that reflect the goodness we wish to see in the world.

Navigating the Law of Cause and Effect:
1. **Mindful Decision-Making:** Before taking action, ask yourself, "What are the potential effects of this choice?" This practice fosters a deeper awareness of the consequences of our actions, guiding us to choose paths that contribute positively to our lives and the lives of others.

2. **Intentional Living:** Cultivate a life lived with intention. Recognize that every moment offers an opportunity to make choices that align with your highest values and aspirations. By doing so, you actively shape the course of your life's journey in harmony with the Law of Cause and Effect.

3. **Reflective Observation:** Regularly reflect on the outcomes

of your actions. This reflection is not about judgment or regret but about learning and growth. Understanding the effects of your actions provides invaluable insights, allowing you to make more informed choices moving forward.

4. **Positive Contribution:** Aim to contribute positively to your environment and community. Knowing that your actions can set off a chain of beneficial effects, seek ways to contribute kindness, support, and positive energy. These contributions ripple outward, touching lives and creating a cycle of positivity that returns to you in kind.

5. **Acceptance and Adaptation:** Recognize that not all outcomes are within your control. While you can guide the causes you create, the effects are often influenced by factors beyond your immediate influence. In these moments, practice acceptance and adaptability, trusting that even unexpected outcomes can lead to new paths of growth and discovery.

To harness the Law of Cause and Effect in shaping a life of intention and proactive decision-making, it's essential to adopt strategies that ground our choices in awareness and purpose. Here are some strategies to become more proactive and intentional in your decision-making process:

1. Define Your Core Values and Principles:
Begin by clearly defining your core values and principles. These serve as your compass, guiding your decisions towards paths that align with

your deepest beliefs and aspirations. Regularly revisit these values, ensuring your choices consistently reflect them.

2. Set Clear Goals and Intentions:

Articulate clear, specific goals and intentions for different areas of your life—be it personal growth, career, relationships, or health. Setting goals gives direction to your actions and decisions, making it easier to identify which choices will lead you closer to your desired outcomes.

3. Practice Mindful Awareness:

Cultivate a practice of mindful awareness in your daily life. By becoming more present and attentive to the here and now, you enhance your ability to make decisions consciously instead of reacting impulsively. Mindfulness can also help you recognize the potential long-term effects of your choices.

4. Embrace Reflective Decision-Making:

Before making a decision, take a moment to reflect. Consider the potential consequences of each option, asking how they align with your values, goals, and the well-being of others involved. Reflective decision-making encourages you to look beyond immediate gains towards more meaningful, lasting benefits.

5. Seek Knowledge and Diverse Perspectives:

Informed decisions are grounded in a thorough understanding of the situation and its possible outcomes. Seek out information and diverse perspectives to broaden your understanding. This can reveal new possibilities and help you anticipate the effects of your choices more accurately.

6. Develop Emotional Intelligence:

Emotional intelligence—the ability to understand and manage your emotions and those of others—plays a crucial role in decision-making. By recognizing and regulating your emotional responses, you can make choices that are driven by reason and aligned with your long-term goals rather than fleeting emotional impulses.

7. Implement a Decision-Making Process:

Adopt a structured process for making significant decisions. This might involve identifying the decision to be made, gathering relevant information, weighing the alternatives, and considering their implications. A systematic approach can reduce the overwhelm and increase the likelihood of making choices that yield positive outcomes.

8. Learn from Past Decisions:

View every decision as a learning opportunity. Reflect on past choices, considering what worked, what didn't, and why. This reflective practice can sharpen your decision-making skills, helping you to make more informed and proactive choices in the future.

9. Cultivate Patience and Trust in the Process:

Recognize that not all decisions will have immediate outcomes. Some effects unfold over time. Cultivate patience and trust in the process, understanding that being proactive and intentional is about playing the long game, focusing on sustained growth and fulfillment.

10. Stay Flexible and Open to Adjustments:

Finally, remain adaptable. Life is dynamic, and what may seem like the best decision now could change with new information or circumstances. Being willing to adjust your course as needed is a sign of strength and wisdom, not indecision.

By integrating these strategies into your approach to decision-making, you empower yourself to make choices that not only lead to beneficial outcomes but also contribute to the unfolding of a life that is truly reflective of who you are and aspire to be.

Chapter Six

The Law of Perpetual Transmutation of Energy

This profound principle reveals that energy, the very substrate of the cosmos, is in a constant state of motion and transformation. Nothing in the universe remains static; all that exists is in a perpetual state of flux, moving from one form to another, from potential to manifestation.

The Fluidity of Energy:

At its core, this law illuminates the fluidity and adaptability of energy. Just as water flows from the mountain to the sea, shifting and shaping itself to the contours of the land, so too does energy move and mold itself to the contours of our thoughts, emotions, and intentions. It is a reminder that the energy within and around us is not fixed but is responsive to our inner states and the vibrations we emit.

The Transformative Power of Intention:

The Law of Perpetual Transmutation of Energy underscores the transformative power of intention. Our intentions act as the mold through which energy flows and takes shape, creating the reality we experience. By harnessing our intentions with clarity and purpose, we direct the flow of energy to manifest our desires and aspirations.

Cultivating Positive Energy:

Understanding this law invites us to become conscious gardeners of our energetic field. Just as a gardener tends to their soil, planting seeds and nurturing their growth, we too can cultivate an environment conducive to the positive transmutation of energy. By nourishing our minds with uplifting thoughts, surrounding ourselves with positive influences, and engaging in actions that resonate with our highest selves, we foster an energetic landscape where our highest potentials can flourish.

Navigating Energy Shifts:
The Law of Perpetual Transmutation of Energy also teaches us to navigate the inevitable shifts and changes in our lives with grace and resilience. Recognizing that energy is always moving and transforming helps us to embrace change rather than resist it. It encourages us to see the potential for growth and renewal in every moment, understanding that even challenging circumstances can be transmuted into opportunities for evolution.

Practical Applications:

- **Mindful Awareness:** Cultivate a practice of mindful awareness to become attuned to the energy you are generating and interacting with. This awareness allows you to consciously choose thoughts and emotions that uplift and support your desired outcomes.

- **Visualization:** Engage in visualization exercises to actively shape the flow of energy. Visualize your goals and desires as already fulfilled, feeling the emotions associated with these achievements. This practice helps to align your energetic frequency with that of your aspirations, facilitating their manifestation.

- **Energy Clearing:** Regularly clear your energetic space through practices such as meditation, spending time in nature, or using sage smudging. Clearing away stagnant or negative energy allows for fresh, positive energy to enter and support your process of transmutation.

- **Gratitude Practice:** Incorporate gratitude into your daily routine. Gratitude elevates your vibration and attracts more of what you appreciate into your life. By focusing on what you are thankful for, you transmute your energetic state to one of abundance and joy.

Transforming negative energy into positive energy is a pivotal aspect of navigating life's challenges and enhancing overall well-being. Here are practical strategies to facilitate this transformation across various dimensions of life:

1. Personal Mindset:

- **Practice Reframing:** Actively change your perspective on difficult situations. Look for the silver lining or the lesson to be learned. This shift in perspective can turn challenges into opportunities for growth.

- **Affirmations:** Use positive affirmations to counteract negative thoughts. Repeating affirmations like "I am capable of overcoming any challenge" can help rewire your brain to focus on strength and resilience.

2. Emotional Well-being:

- **Emotional Release:** Allow yourself to feel and express your emotions in healthy ways, such as through writing, art, or physical activity. Releasing pent-up emotions can prevent them from manifesting as negative energy.

- **Seek Joy:** Make time for activities that bring you happiness and fulfillment. Joy is a powerful antidote to negativity, uplifting your spirit and those around you.

3. Relationships:

- **Communication:** Address conflicts and misunderstandings with open and honest communication. Holding onto resentment can create negative energy, while resolving issues can lead to stronger, more positive connections.

- **Surround Yourself with Positivity:** Spend time with people who uplift and support you. Their positive energy can help diminish the impact of negativity in your life.

4. Work and Career:

- **Set Boundaries:** Establish clear boundaries to protect your energy. Knowing when to say no or to take a break can prevent burnout and keep your work environment more positive.

- **Find Meaning:** Seek out aspects of your work that you find meaningful. Engaging in tasks that align with your values and goals can transform your outlook on your job and increase job satisfaction.

5. Physical Health:

- **Exercise Regularly:** Physical activity releases endorphins, which have mood-boosting properties. A healthy body can influence a positive mindset.

- **Nutrition:** Eating a balanced diet rich in nutrients can have a profound effect on your mood and energy levels. Foods that are high in vitamins, minerals, and antioxidants can help combat stress and negativity.

6. Spiritual Practice:

- **Meditation and Mindfulness:** Regular meditation or mindfulness practice can help you detach from negative thoughts and emotions, allowing you to observe them without judgment and let them go.

- **Connect with Nature:** Spending time in nature can be incredibly grounding and can help clear negative energy, replacing it with a sense of peace and renewal.

7. Home Environment:

- **Declutter:** A cluttered space can reflect and amplify negative energy. Regularly decluttering your living space can create a more peaceful and positive environment.

- **Incorporate Nature:** Bringing elements of nature into your home, such as plants or natural light, can enhance the positive energy of your space.

8. Contribution and Service:

- **Give Back:** Volunteering or helping others can shift your focus from your own problems to the act of making a positive difference in the world, thereby reducing negative feelings and fostering a sense of purpose.

Visualization and meditation are potent practices for experiencing the transmutation of energy from negative to positive. These exercises can help shift your internal state, promoting a sense of peace, clarity, and renewed energy. Here are some guided steps to incorporate these practices into your routine for energy transmutation:

1. Grounding Meditation:

- **Find a Quiet Space:** Begin by finding a quiet and comfortable place where you won't be disturbed.

- **Relax Your Body:** Sit or lie down in a comfortable position. Close your eyes and take several deep breaths, focusing on relaxing each part of your body from your toes to the crown of your head.

- **Visualize Roots:** Imagine roots extending from the base of your spine or feet, growing deep into the earth. Visualize these roots drawing up stabilizing and nourishing energy from the earth into your body with each inhale.

- **Release Negative Energy:** As you exhale, visualize any negative energy, stress, or tension leaving your body through the roots and being neutralized by the earth.

- **Cycle of Energy:** Continue this cycle of drawing in positive energy and releasing negative energy for several minutes until you feel grounded and centered.

2. Light Visualization Exercise:

- **Prepare:** In a relaxed seated position, close your eyes and breathe deeply to center yourself.

- **Envision Healing Light:** Picture a brilliant, healing light above your head. This light can be any color that resonates with you. Imagine it as a source of pure, positive energy.

- **Fill With Light:** Visualize this light slowly descending over you, entering through the crown of your head and filling your entire body. See or feel this light as it transmutes any negative thoughts, emotions, or physical sensations into positive, radiant energy.

- **Expand the Light:** Continue to visualize this light expanding beyond the boundaries of your body, creating a protective and nourishing aura around you. Sit with this sensation for as long as you like.

3. Energy Flow Meditation:
- **Begin With Breath:** Start by focusing on your breath, allowing yourself to become fully present. With each inhale, gather up any negative or stagnant energy within you.

- **Visualize Transmutation:** As you exhale, imagine this negative energy being transformed into positive energy—perhaps seeing it change color or brightness.

- **Direct the Energy:** Now, envision directing this positive energy to areas of your life that need healing or improvement. Imagine these areas being bathed in this transformative light, experiencing renewal and growth.

- **Closure:** Gradually bring your focus back to the present moment, carrying the sensation of refreshed and positive energy with you.

4. Heart Coherence Exercise:
- **Focus on the Heart:** Close your eyes, and focus your attention on your heart area. Breathe slowly and deeply, imagining your breath flowing in and out of your heart.

- **Activate Positive Emotions:** Recall a positive experience or feeling—love, gratitude, joy—and try to re-experience it as fully as possible, focusing on the sensation in your heart area.

- **Expand and Share:** Visualize this positive emotion as energy that grows with each breath, filling your entire body and then expanding outward. Imagine this energy touching the lives of people around you, spreading positivity and harmony.

Incorporating these visualization and meditation exercises into your daily routine can significantly impact your ability to transmute negative energy into positive, enhancing your overall well-being and your ability to navigate life's challenges with grace and resilience.

Chapter Seven

The Law of Attraction

This magnetic law governs the cosmic order, dictating that the energy we emit through our thoughts, feelings, and beliefs invariably draws similar energy towards us. It's the universe's way of matching our vibrational frequency, mirroring back to us the essence of our inner world.

Understanding the Magnetic Power of Thought:

At the heart of the Law of Attraction lies the power of thought. Our thoughts are not merely reflections of our inner state; they are active energy frequencies that interact with the fabric of reality. Positive thoughts vibrate at a high frequency, attracting circumstances, people, and experiences that resonate with positivity. Conversely, dwelling on negative thoughts lowers our vibrational frequency, attracting negativity into our lives. This principle underscores the importance of cultivating a mindset that aligns with the outcomes we desire.

Emotional Guidance System:

Our emotions serve as a compass, guiding us through the Law of Attraction. They indicate the vibrational frequency we're currently emitting. Feelings of joy, love, and gratitude signal that we're in alignment with our desires, effectively attracting positive manifestations. In contrast, emotions like fear, anger, and despair suggest a misalignment, pulling us away from our aspirations. By becoming attuned to our emotions, we can adjust our vibrational output to better match the frequency of our desires.

Visualization as a Tool for Manifestation:

Visualization is a powerful technique for harnessing the Law of Attraction. By vividly imagining ourselves achieving our goals, we energetically align with those outcomes. This practice involves more than just picturing success; it requires feeling the emotions associated with that success, thereby amplifying our vibrational frequency to match what we wish to attract.

Affirmations and Declarations:

Affirmations are positive statements that reinforce our desired reality. When repeated with conviction, affirmations help reshape our subconscious beliefs, aligning our thought patterns with the frequency of our goals. Declarations of intent, spoken aloud, act as a powerful signal to the universe, setting the Law of Attraction into motion.

Taking Inspired Action:

While the Law of Attraction emphasizes the power of thought and emotion, it also necessitates action. However, this is not about taking any action but rather inspired action that feels aligned with our goals. Such actions are not forced but flow naturally from a state of positive alignment, further reinforcing our intentions and attracting the desired outcomes with greater ease.

Cultivating Gratitude:

Gratitude amplifies the Law of Attraction by focusing on abundance rather than lack. By appreciating what we already have, we elevate our vibrational frequency, attracting more of what we're grateful for. It's a cycle of positivity that fuels itself, transforming our perspective and our life experience.

Maintaining Alignment:

The key to effectively utilizing the Law of Attraction lies in maintaining alignment between our thoughts, emotions, and actions. This alignment ensures that we emit a clear, consistent vibrational signal that resonates with our desires. Regular self-reflection, meditation, and mindfulness practices can help maintain this alignment, keeping us on the path to manifesting our goals.

Harnessing the Law of Attraction through focused intention and feeling involves cultivating a deep, resonant connection between what we desire and the vibrational energy we emit. The following guided practices are designed to bridge this connection, transforming desires into tangible realities:

1. The Clarity Map:

- **Define Your Desire:** Start with a clear and specific definition of what you desire. Whether it's a goal, a feeling, or an experience, clarity is key. Write it down in detail.

- **Visualize with Feeling:** Close your eyes and visualize yourself achieving this desire. Imagine the scene in vivid detail—where are you, who is with you, what are you doing? Most importantly, immerse yourself in the feeling of having achieved this desire. What emotions are you experiencing? Joy, gratitude, peace?

- **Daily Reinforcement:** Dedicate a few minutes each day to this visualization practice, each time focusing on the sensory details and emotions involved. This repetition reinforces your intention and aligns your vibrational frequency with your desire.

2. The Emotional Alchemist:

- **Identify Your Emotional State:** Acknowledge your current emotional state regarding your desire. If there are feelings of doubt, fear, or impatience, recognize them without judgment.

- **Transformative Breathing:** Take deep, slow breaths. With each inhale, visualize drawing in positive energy filled with possibility and hope. With each exhale, imagine releasing any negative emotions or doubts.

- **Elevate Your Emotion:** Shift your focus to the feeling of your desire already being fulfilled. Cultivate emotions like joy, gratitude, and love, allowing them to permeate your being. This practice transmutes lower vibrational emotions into higher ones, aligning you with your desire.

3. The Affirmation Anchor:

- **Craft Affirmations:** Create a set of positive affirmations that reflect your desire as already achieved. Use the present tense, such as "I am living in abundance," or "I am surrounded by loving relationships."

- **Incorporate into Routine:** Integrate these affirmations into your daily routine. Repeat them out loud each morning, write them in your journal, or post them where you'll see them throughout the day.

- **Embody the Affirmations:** As you engage with these affirmations, do more than just recite them—strive to embody the feelings they represent. Feel the truth of these affirmations as if they are your current reality.

4. The Gratitude Gateway:

- **Daily Gratitude Practice:** Each day, list at least three things you're grateful for, related to your desire or otherwise. This practice shifts your focus from lack to abundance, raising your vibrational frequency.

- **Gratitude Visualization:** Occasionally, visualize a future moment where you're expressing gratitude for having achieved your desire. This future-focused gratitude further strengthens the energetic connection to your desire.

5. The Inspired Action Plan:

- **Listen for Inspiration:** Pay attention to any inspirations or intuitive nudges that relate to your desire. The Law of Attraction often works through inspired action—steps that feel naturally compelling.

- **Take Action:** Act on these inspirations, no matter how small or inconsequential they may seem. Each action is a co-creation with the universe, bringing you closer to your desire.

- **Reflect on Alignment:** Regularly check in with yourself to ensure your actions feel aligned with your desire. If something feels off, reassess and realign your actions with your intention.

6. The Synchronicity Journal:

- **Record Synchronicities:** Keep a journal of any synchronicities, serendipitous events, or "coincidences" that occur related to your desire. These are often signs that you're in alignment with your desire's vibrational frequency.

- **Reflect on Connections:** Periodically review your journal entries to reflect on the connections and progress toward your desire. This reflection can reinforce your belief in the Law of Attraction and your ability to manifest your desires.

Through these guided practices, you actively engage with the Law of Attraction, utilizing focused intention and emotion to draw your desires into your lived experience. Remember, the key is consistency, faith, and an open heart, ready to receive and embrace the manifestations of your deepest aspirations.

Chapter Eight

The Law of Rhythm

The Law of Rhythm speaks to the universal truth that life moves in cycles, much like the ebb and flow of the tides or the changing of the seasons. This law teaches us that everything in the universe follows a natural rhythm or pattern—growth and decline, rise and fall, movement and rest. It is a reminder that our lives, too, are governed by these cycles, with periods of activity and growth followed by times of rest and introspection.

Understanding Life's Natural Cycles:

Life's natural cycles are evident in the world around us and within our own experiences. Just as the earth experiences spring's growth, summer's abundance, autumn's harvest, and winter's rest, we too undergo phases of expansion, fruition, reflection, and renewal. Recognizing and respecting these cycles encourages us to work with them, rather than against them, allowing for a more harmonious existence.

Flowing with the Rhythm:

Flowing with the Law of Rhythm means embracing the changes and cycles in our lives with grace and flexibility. It involves understanding that periods of challenge or perceived stagnation are not setbacks but natural phases of our growth and evolution. By tuning into our own personal rhythms, we can better anticipate and prepare for these cycles, making conscious choices that align with our current phase of life.

Practical Ways to Harmonize with Life's Rhythms:

1. **Mindful Observation:** Become an observer of nature and your own life. Notice the rhythms present in the natural world and reflect on the cycles you experience personally—energy levels, creativity, moods. This awareness can guide you to make decisions that are in harmony with your current cycle.

2. **Embrace Change:** Accept that change is a natural and nec-

essary part of life's rhythm. Rather than resisting change, welcome it as an opportunity for growth and renewal. Trust that each phase, whether it appears positive or challenging, serves a purpose in your personal development.

3. **Balance Activity with Rest:** Recognize the importance of balancing periods of activity with times of rest. Just as the earth lies fallow in winter to prepare for the growth of spring, allowing yourself time to rest and reflect is essential for your growth and well-being.

4. **Set Intentions with the Seasons:** Use the changing seasons as a guide for setting intentions and goals. For example, spring is a time for planting new seeds (ideas or projects), while autumn may be a time for harvesting and reflection on what you've accomplished.

5. **Cultivate Flexibility:** Develop an attitude of flexibility and adaptability. Understand that life's rhythm may bring unexpected changes, and being flexible allows you to navigate these with resilience and grace.

6. **Celebrate the Cycles:** Create rituals or practices to celebrate the completion of a cycle and the beginning of a new one. This could be a personal ritual to mark achievements and transitions or celebrating traditional seasonal festivals that honor nature's cycles.

The Gift of Rhythm:

The Law of Rhythm offers a profound gift—the understanding that our lives are part of a greater cosmic dance. By embracing this law, we learn to move gracefully through life's cycles, aligning our actions with the natural flow of the universe. This alignment brings a sense of peace and fulfillment, as we understand that we are never truly stagnant but always in motion, part of the eternal rhythm of life.

Adapting to and embracing life's inherent ebbs and flows is crucial for achieving harmony and contentment. Here are practical suggestions to help you navigate and make the most of these natural rhythms:

1. Practice Mindful Acceptance:
- Cultivate a mindset of acceptance towards the natural cycles of life. Acknowledge that both highs and lows are essential and transient phases. Mindfulness meditation can be particularly effective in developing an attitude of acceptance, helping you to observe life's changes without judgment.

2. Adjust Your Pace:
- Recognize when to accelerate your efforts and when to slow down. Just as farmers understand the importance of sowing seeds at the right time and resting in the off-season, learn to adjust your pace according to the rhythm of your life. This might mean pushing forward with projects when your energy is high and allowing yourself to rest and reflect when it's not.

3. Establish Flexible Routines:
- While maintaining a routine can provide stability, flexibility allows you to adapt to life's changing rhythms. Create routines that have room for adjustment, so you can respond to your needs and external circumstances without feeling overwhelmed or rigid.

4. Cultivate Resilience in the Face of Change:

- Build your emotional and psychological resilience by adopting a growth mindset. View challenges as opportunities to learn and grow. Techniques such as journaling about past challenges you've overcome can remind you of your resilience and help you face current and future changes with confidence.

5. Engage in Reflective Practices:

- Regular reflection can help you understand your personal cycles and patterns. Set aside time for practices like journaling, reflective walking, or quiet contemplation to gain insights into how you best navigate periods of change.

6. Embrace Self-Compassion:

- Be kind to yourself during difficult times. Recognize that it's okay to feel unsettled by life's ebbs and flows. Self-compassion practices, such as speaking to yourself with kindness and understanding your common humanity, can provide comfort and reassurance.

7. Seek Support and Community:

- Sharing your experiences with trusted friends, family, or support groups can provide perspective and solace. Connection with others can remind you that you're not alone in navigating life's ups and downs.

8. Celebrate the Cycles:

- Create personal rituals or celebrations that acknowledge the completion of one cycle and the beginning of another. This could be as simple as a quiet moment of gratitude at the end of a challenging period or celebrating achievements, big or small.

9. Stay Connected to Nature:

- Aligning with the natural world can help you resonate with the concept of cycles. Spending time in nature, observing the changing seasons, and the rhythms of the natural world can be a powerful reminder of life's broader cycles and rhythms.

10. Prioritize Adaptability:

- Develop skills and hobbies that allow you to adapt to changing circumstances. This could mean diversifying your skill set in your professional life or engaging in hobbies that can be enjoyed in various settings and seasons of life.

Engaging in reflective practices allows for a deeper connection with both personal and universal rhythms, facilitating a harmonious alignment with the cyclical nature of existence. Here are some reflective practices designed to help you identify and align with these rhythms:

1. Journaling for Self-Discovery:

- **Daily Reflections:** Dedicate time each day to reflect on your experiences, emotions, and reactions. Note any patterns that emerge, such as times of day when you feel most energetic or creative and periods when you need rest.

- **Cycle Tracking:** Keep track of personal cycles, such as productivity cycles, emotional cycles, and even physical cycles. Observe how these may correlate with external cycles, like the phases of the moon or seasonal changes.

2. Meditation on Natural Cycles:

- **Guided Visualization:** Engage in guided meditations that focus on the imagery of natural cycles, such as the rising and setting of the sun, the phases of the moon, or the changing seasons. Visualize yourself as part of these cycles, flowing seamlessly with them.

- **Mindfulness Meditation:** Practice mindfulness meditation to enhance your awareness of the present moment. This practice can heighten your sensitivity to the subtle shifts in energy and rhythm within and around you.

3. Rhythmic Breathing Exercises:

- **Conscious Breathing:** Incorporate breathing exercises that mimic natural rhythms, such as the ebb and flow of waves or the cyclical pattern of breathing found in many living beings. This can help synchronize your personal rhythm with wider natural rhythms.

4. Nature Immersion:

- **Regular Time Outdoors:** Spend time in nature to directly experience and connect with the natural world's rhythms. Whether it's a daily walk in the park or occasional trips to more secluded natural settings, this direct engagement can be profoundly aligning.

- **Nature Observation:** Actively observe the rhythms in nature, from the lifecycle of plants to the behavior of animals throughout the seasons. This observation can offer insights into the universal rhythms that also influence human life.

5. Creative Expression:

- **Artistic Exploration:** Use art, music, writing, or dance to explore and express your personal rhythms. Creative activities can be a powerful medium for connecting with and articulating the rhythms you experience internally and observe externally.

- **Creative Rituals:** Establish creative rituals that align with natural cycles, such as drawing a new picture with each new moon or writing a poem to mark the changing seasons.

6. **Cycle Synthesis:**
   - **Integration Activities:** Once you've identified personal and natural cycles, engage in activities that consciously align these rhythms. For example, plan more demanding tasks during your personal high-energy phases while scheduling rest during lower-energy times.

   - **Alignment Reflections:** Reflect on how aligning your personal rhythm with universal cycles affects your well-being, productivity, and sense of harmony. Adjust your practices as needed to enhance this alignment.

7. **Seasonal Goal Setting:**
   - **Align Goals with Seasons:** Set personal goals and intentions that resonate with the energy of the current season. For example, focus on growth and new projects in the spring, fruition and celebration in the summer, reflection and gratitude in the autumn, and rest and renewal in the winter.

   - **Seasonal Reviews:** At the end of each season, review your achievements and challenges. Reflect on how the season's energy supported or hindered your goals and how you can better align your activities with the coming season's rhythm.

By incorporating these reflective practices into your routine, you become more attuned to the rhythms that govern life. This attunement fosters a deeper sense of connection with yourself and the world around you, enabling you to move through life with greater ease, resilience, and fulfillment.

Chapter Nine

The Law of Compensation

This law, deeply rooted in the concept of cause and effect, extends beyond mere financial or material gain, encompassing the broader spectrum of actions, intentions, and energies we put forth into the world. It teaches us that for every effort, there is an equal or greater return, not always in the form we expect but in a manner that the universe deems most fitting and beneficial for our growth.

The Essence of Balance:

At the heart of the Law of Compensation is the understanding that the universe operates on a principle of equilibrium. Just as nature strives for balance within ecosystems, so too does this law work to maintain a cosmic balance, ensuring that nothing goes unrewarded or unnoticed. Whether it's kindness, hard work, creativity, or love, every positive action generates a ripple of positive energy, which the universe eventually returns in kind.

Beyond Material Compensation:

While it's easy to equate compensation with material rewards, the Law of Compensation encompasses much more. It includes love, friendships, opportunities, experiences, and insights gained. This broader perspective invites us to look beyond immediate or tangible returns, recognizing the intrinsic value in acts of generosity, perseverance, and integrity.

Aligning Actions with Desired Compensation:

To harmonize with the Law of Compensation, it's crucial to align our actions with the type of compensation we seek. This alignment involves:

- **Intentionality:** Acting with clear, positive intentions increases the likelihood of attracting desirable outcomes. The purity and strength of our intentions directly influence the quality and magnitude of the compensation we receive.

- **Generosity:** The act of giving without the expectation of return paradoxically opens the channels for receiving. By contributing positively to the lives of others, we set the stage for reciprocal blessings, often in unexpected ways.

- **Personal Growth:** Viewing challenges as opportunities for learning and growth can transform potential setbacks into valuable experiences, which are a form of compensation in their own right. The wisdom and strength gained through adversity are invaluable rewards that propel us forward on our journey.

Practical Applications:
- **Gratitude Practice:** Cultivate a daily practice of gratitude to acknowledge and appreciate the myriad ways the universe compensates you. This practice can shift your focus from what you lack to the abundance you already possess, attracting more positivity into your life.

- **Conscious Contribution:** Seek opportunities to contribute positively to your community and the world at large. Whether through volunteering, mentoring, or simple acts of kindness, these contributions are seeds that will grow and return to you manifold.

- **Reflective Assessment:** Regularly reflect on the relationship between your actions and the compensation you receive. This introspection can provide insights into how you might adjust your actions to better align with the rewards you desire.

Fostering a mindset and taking actions that invite positive compensation from the universe involves cultivating certain attitudes and behaviors that align with the Law of Compensation. Here are strategies to help you create an environment within yourself and in your life that attracts the kind of returns you desire:

1. Cultivate a Positive Mindset:

- **Focus on Abundance:** Shift your perspective from a scarcity mindset to one of abundance. Believe that there is enough for everyone and that you deserve to receive as much as anyone else. This belief opens you up to receive the universe's bounty.

- **Visualize Success:** Regularly visualize achieving your goals and receiving the rewards you seek. Imagine the feelings of joy, satisfaction, and gratitude that come with these achievements. This visualization practice aligns your energy with the outcomes you desire.

2. Practice Gratitude:

- **Daily Gratitude:** Start or end your day by listing things you're grateful for. Acknowledging the good in your life, no matter how small, attracts more positive experiences and is a form of compensation in itself.

- **Gratitude in Challenges:** Find something to be grateful for even in difficult situations. This practice can transmute negative energy into positive, inviting constructive compensation.

3. Give Generously:

- **Give Without Expectation:** Offer your time, resources, or talents freely without expecting anything in return. The act of giving selflessly increases your vibrational frequency and invites positive compensation from unexpected sources.

- **Diversify Your Giving:** Extend your generosity not just to individuals but to the community and the environment. The wider your positive impact, the broader the channels through which compensation can return to you.

4. Engage in Personal Growth:

- **Continuous Learning:** View life as a continuous learning journey. Seek out opportunities for growth, education, and self-improvement. The knowledge and wisdom you gain are valuable forms of compensation that can enhance all areas of your life.

- **Overcome Challenges:** Approach challenges as opportunities to grow stronger and wiser. Each obstacle overcome is a step toward becoming a better version of yourself, which is a profound form of compensation.

5. Maintain Integrity:

- **Align Actions with Values:** Ensure your actions and decisions are in alignment with your core values. Living authentically and ethically attracts positive experiences and relationships into your life.

- **Be Accountable:** Take responsibility for your actions and their outcomes. Owning up to mistakes and learning from them fosters trust and respect, which are valuable compensations in their own right.

6. Build Positive Relationships:

- **Cultivate Supportive Networks:** Surround yourself with positive, supportive people who uplift and encourage you. The love, support, and guidance of friends and family are invaluable forms of compensation.

- **Be a Positive Force:** Strive to be someone who brings positivity into the lives of others. The goodwill you create often comes back to you manifold.

7. Stay Open and Receptive:

- **Be Open to Various Forms of Compensation:** Recognize that compensation can come in many forms—opportunities, relationships, insights, and material benefits. Stay open and grateful for all forms of positive return.

- **Trust the Universe:** Have faith that the universe will provide for you in the best way possible at the right time. This trust removes resistance and allows you to receive more freely.

Practicing gratitude and generosity can significantly enhance your ability to attract positive compensation according to the Law of Compensation. Here are activities designed to deepen your practice of these virtues, enriching not only your life but also those around you:

1. Gratitude Journaling:

- **Daily Entries:** Make it a habit to write down three to five things you're grateful for each day. Try to be specific and include a variety of aspects from different areas of your life.

- **Gratitude Reflection:** Once a week, review your entries and reflect on the abundance in your life. This practice can deepen your appreciation and awareness of the good surrounding you.

2. Generosity Challenges:

- **Random Acts of Kindness:** Set yourself a challenge to perform a certain number of random acts of kindness each week. These can range from paying for someone's coffee to volunteering your time for a cause you care about.

- **Gift of Time:** Dedicate a portion of your time to help someone else, whether it's offering to tutor a student, helping a neighbor with chores, or lending an ear to a friend in need.

3. Gratitude Meditation:

- **Focused Meditation:** Spend a few minutes each day in meditation, focusing on the feeling of gratitude. Visualize the things you're grateful for and allow the feeling of appreciation to fill your entire being.

- **Sending Gratitude:** During your meditation, also focus on sending gratitude out to the universe, to people in your life, and even to those you've had challenges with.

4. Generosity Jar:

- **Setting Up:** Place a jar in a common area of your home and fill it with small notes of generosity ideas or acts of kindness you can perform.

- **Acting on It:** Regularly draw an idea from the jar and act on it. This can be a fun and spontaneous way to integrate generosity into your daily life.

5. Gratitude Visits:
- **Writing Letters:** Write gratitude letters to people who have made a positive impact on your life. Be specific about what you're thankful for and the difference they've made.

- **Delivering in Person:** If possible, deliver these letters in person and take the time to read them out loud to the recipient. This can be a powerful experience for both you and the person you're thanking.

6. Generosity of Spirit:
- **Compliment Generously:** Make it a point to give genuine compliments daily. Recognizing and vocalizing the positive qualities and achievements of others can uplift their spirits and yours.

- **Share Knowledge and Resources:** If you have expertise or resources that could benefit others, share them freely. This could mean mentoring someone, sharing useful information, or donating to those in need.

7. Gratitude Affirmations:
- **Creating Affirmations:** Write a list of gratitude affirmations that resonate with you, such as "I am deeply thankful for the abundance in my life" or "I appreciate every person

and every experience that has shaped me."

- **Daily Practice:** Repeat these affirmations to yourself, especially during moments of stress or challenge. This can help shift your focus back to a state of appreciation.

8. Pay It Forward:

- **Acts of Forward Generosity:** When someone does something kind for you, instead of paying them back, 'pay it forward' by doing something kind for someone else. This creates a ripple effect of generosity and kindness in the community.

Incorporating these activities into your daily routine can significantly shift your focus towards gratitude and generosity, key components that amplify the Law of Compensation in your life. By actively practicing these virtues, you not only enhance your own vibrational frequency but also contribute to a more positive and abundant world.

Chapter Ten

The Law of Relativity

This universal law suggests that nothing in our lives is inherently good or bad, big or small, easy or difficult until it is compared with something else. It is through this comparison that we give meaning and context to our experiences, shaping our perception of the world around us.

The Power of Perspective:

The essence of the Law of Relativity lies in the understanding that our perspective—how we choose to view situations, events, and experiences—greatly influences our reality. A challenging situation viewed from one angle can be seen as an opportunity for growth from another. By shifting our perspective, we can transform our experience of reality, finding value and meaning in even the most difficult circumstances.

Subjectivity of Experiences:

Our experiences are deeply personal and subjective, colored by our beliefs, past experiences, and expectations. What one person perceives as a setback, another might see as a stepping stone. This subjectivity highlights the importance of recognizing and respecting the diversity of experiences and perspectives that each person brings to the table.

Practical Applications of the Law of Relativity:

1. **Cultivate Empathy and Understanding:** Recognize that everyone's experience is relative to their unique life circumstances. Practice empathy by putting yourself in others' shoes, striving to understand their perspective. This can foster deeper connections and reduce conflicts.

2. **Reframe Challenges:** When faced with challenges, actively reframe them in a relative context. Ask yourself, "Compared to what?" This question can help you see that what might feel like a major issue in the moment may be minor in the grand

scheme of things, or that it could have been much worse, which can bring a sense of relief and gratitude.

3. **Celebrate Personal Progress:** Instead of comparing your progress or success to others, use your past self as the benchmark. This application of the Law of Relativity focuses on your growth and achievements, fostering a positive self-image and motivation to continue evolving.

4. **Maintain a Balanced Perspective:** Practice balancing your perspective by considering multiple viewpoints. This can help you develop a more nuanced understanding of life's experiences, reducing the tendency to label them as purely good or bad.

5. **Embrace Diversity of Thought:** Encourage and embrace different perspectives, whether in conversations, in the workplace, or in social settings. Recognizing the value in diverse viewpoints can broaden your understanding and appreciation of the world.

6. **Mindful Consumption of Media:** Be mindful of how media can influence your perception of reality. Seek out diverse sources of information to gain a more balanced and relative understanding of events and issues.

Personal Growth Through Relativity:

The Law of Relativity serves as a powerful tool for personal growth and enlightenment. By understanding and applying this law, we learn to see life's experiences not as isolated incidents but as part of a broader, relative landscape. This perspective encourages us to find meaning, learn from each experience, and cultivate a more compassionate, empathetic, and balanced view of life.

Embracing challenges as opportunities for growth is a transformative approach that aligns with the Law of Relativity. By shifting our perspective, we can extract valuable lessons from obstacles and use them as stepping stones for personal development. Here are techniques to help you use challenges as catalysts for growth:

1. Adopt a Growth Mindset:

- **Embrace Learning:** View challenges as opportunities to learn something new about yourself, others, or the world. This mindset encourages resilience and openness to experience.

- **Celebrate Effort:** Focus on the effort and progress made, rather than solely on the outcome. Recognize that growth often comes from the journey, not just the destination.

2. Practice Reflective Journaling:

- **Document Challenges:** Write about the challenges you face, describing them in detail. This process can help externalize the problem and may reduce its perceived intensity.

- **Identify Lessons:** For each challenge, reflect on and write down the lessons learned or the strengths you developed as a result. Over time, this journal can serve as a powerful reminder of your resilience and growth.

3. Set Specific Growth Goals:

- **Identify Areas for Development:** Use challenges as a mirror to reflect on areas of your life or character that could benefit from improvement or strengthening.

- **Create Actionable Steps:** For each area identified, set specific, measurable goals for how you can grow or improve. Break these down into actionable steps to make progress tangible.

4. Seek Feedback and Support:

- **Reach Out for Perspectives:** Discuss your challenges with trusted friends, mentors, or advisors. Others can offer valuable perspectives, insights, or advice that you might not have considered.

- **Build a Support Network:** Surround yourself with people who encourage growth and provide constructive feedback. This network can offer encouragement and accountability as you work through challenges.

5. Engage in Problem-Solving Activities:

- **Brainstorm Solutions:** When faced with a challenge, take time to brainstorm potential solutions. This exercise can enhance your problem-solving skills and creativity.

- **Implement and Reflect:** Choose a solution to implement, then reflect on the process and outcome. What worked well? What could be improved? This cycle of action and reflection fosters adaptability and learning.

6. Practice Mindfulness and Stress Reduction:

- **Mindfulness Meditation:** Engage in mindfulness practices to cultivate a calm, centered state of mind. This can help you approach challenges with clarity and reduce reactive emotional responses.

- **Stress-Reduction Techniques:** Utilize stress-reduction techniques, such as deep breathing, yoga, or physical exercise, to maintain equilibrium in the face of challenges.

7. Cultivate Gratitude for Challenges:

- **Gratitude Reflection:** Regularly reflect on how specific challenges have contributed to your growth. Cultivating gratitude for these experiences can transform your perception of obstacles into appreciation for the opportunities they provide.

8. Embrace Change and Uncertainty:

Flexibility and Openness: Cultivate an attitude of flexibility and openness to change. Recognize that uncertainty can lead to unexpected opportunities for growth and development.

Fostering empathy and contentment through comparative exercises involves engaging in reflective practices that encourage you to see life from different perspectives and appreciate your own journey. These exercises can deepen your understanding of the Law of Relativity by highlighting the subjective nature of experiences and promoting a sense of gratitude and connection with others. Here are some comparative exercises designed to cultivate empathy and contentment:

1. The "In Their Shoes" Reflection:

- **Choose a Perspective:** Think of someone whose life situation is significantly different from yours—this could be a friend facing a challenge, a historical figure, or even a character from a book or movie.

- **Reflect and Write:** Spend some time reflecting on what daily life might be like for this person. Write about the challenges they face, the joys they might experience, and the resilience they show. Try to capture the emotions and motivations behind their actions.

- **Empathy and Gratitude:** Reflect on how this exercise makes you feel about your own circumstances. Identify aspects of your life for which you are grateful and consider how you can show empathy to others in similar situations.

2. The Gratitude Swap:

- **Partner Up:** Pair up with a friend or family member for this exercise. Each person shares something they're currently struggling with.

- **Find the Positive:** Swap perspectives and try to find positive aspects or potential growth opportunities in the other person's challenge. Discuss these perspectives with each other.

- **Reflect:** This exchange can help both parties see their situations in a new light, fostering empathy and highlighting the relativity of challenges and blessings.

3. The Historical Comparison:

- **Research and Reflect:** Choose a historical period or event that interests you. Research the living conditions, societal norms, and individual stories from this time.

- **Compare and Contrast:** Compare your current life circumstances with those you researched. Consider the advancements, opportunities, and freedoms you have today that were not available or were different in the past.

- **Contentment and Appreciation:** Use this comparison to cultivate a deeper appreciation for the present and a sense of contentment with your own life's path.

4. The "Day in the Life" Simulation:

- **Select a Scenario:** Choose a life scenario vastly different from your own. This could involve living with a certain limitation, in a different culture, or under different socioeconomic conditions.

- **Live a Day:** Spend a day (or even just a few hours) simulating this scenario as closely as possible. This could involve changing your routine, limiting your resources, or adopting new practices.

- **Reflect and Empathize:** Reflect on the experience. What insights did you gain about the challenges and strengths in this scenario? How does it affect your empathy for people living in such circumstances and your contentment with your own life?

5. The Contentment Timeline:

- **Create a Timeline:** Draw a timeline of your life, marking significant events, both challenging and joyful.

- **Reflect on Growth:** For each event, reflect on how you felt at the time versus how you view it now. Identify the growth, lessons, or hidden blessings that came from each experience.

- **Gratitude and Perspective:** This visual representation can help you see how challenges have contributed to your growth and how blessings may have been disguised. It fosters a sense of gratitude for your journey and contentment with where you are now.

Engaging in these exercises can significantly enhance your capacity for empathy by allowing you to understand and feel the emotions and experiences of others. Simultaneously, they encourage a deep-seated contentment with your own life by highlighting the unique path you've traveled and the lessons learned along the way. Through comparative reflection, you can cultivate a richer, more empathetic, and contented perspective on life.

Chapter Eleven

The Law of Correspondence

This law encapsulates the idea that the outer world is a mirror reflecting our inner world; our thoughts, emotions, beliefs, and attitudes are manifested in our physical experiences and the environment around us.

The Mirror of the External World:

At its core, the Law of Correspondence suggests that to change our outer experiences, we must first initiate change within ourselves. If we perceive our external reality as chaotic, lacking, or unfulfilling, it prompts us to examine our internal state and identify the corresponding thoughts or beliefs that may be manifesting these conditions. By aligning our inner world with the qualities we wish to see externally, we can effectively transform our life experiences.

Internal States Shaping Reality:

Our internal states—comprising our thoughts, feelings, beliefs, and subconscious programming—serve as the blueprint for our external reality. They influence our actions, attract certain experiences, and shape our interactions with others. This profound connection underscores the importance of cultivating a positive, abundant, and peaceful inner landscape to reflect the same in our external world.

Practical Applications of the Law of Correspondence:

1. Mindfulness and Self-Awareness:

- Cultivate mindfulness and self-awareness to become conscious of your internal dialogue and emotional state. Regular practices such as meditation, journaling, or reflective contemplation can aid in this awareness, helping you to identify and shift negative patterns.

2. Affirmations and Visualization:

- Employ affirmations and visualization techniques to reinforce positive beliefs and outcomes in your mind. By consistently focusing on positive, empowering thoughts, you can start to see these qualities mirrored in your external circumstances.

3. **Emotional Regulation and Healing:**

  - Engage in emotional regulation and healing practices to address and resolve internal conflicts, traumas, or limiting beliefs. Techniques such as therapy, emotional freedom technique (EFT), or even creative expression can facilitate this healing process, leading to positive changes in your external world.

4. **Intentional Living:**

  - Live intentionally by aligning your daily actions, choices, and interactions with the values and outcomes you wish to manifest. This congruence between your internal intentions and external actions reinforces the desired changes in your reality.

5. **Gratitude Practice:**

  - Implement a daily gratitude practice to focus on abundance and positivity. Recognizing and appreciating what you already have creates a vibrational match for attracting more of the same into your life.

6. **Surround Yourself with Positivity:**

  - Curate your environment to reflect the positivity and success you seek. This can involve decluttering your space, surrounding yourself with inspirational people and materials, and creating a physical environment that supports your goals and well-being.

Reflecting Change in the External by Transforming the Internal:

The Law of Correspondence empowers us to take control of our lives by recognizing the power of our internal state to shape our external reality. It calls for a holistic approach to personal development, one that addresses the mind, emotions, and spirit. By consciously working to transform our inner world, we set the stage for meaningful and positive changes in our external experiences, ultimately leading to a more fulfilled and harmonious life.

Aligning one's inner world with desired external outcomes requires a conscious effort to cultivate self-awareness and actively work towards personal transformation. Here are methods designed to facilitate internal reflection and ensure your internal state is in harmony with the goals you wish to achieve in your external reality:

1. **Deep Self-Reflection:**

   - **Set Aside Regular Time:** Dedicate specific times for deep self-reflection, free from distractions. Use this time to meditate, journal, or simply ponder your thoughts, feelings, beliefs, and attitudes.

   - **Questioning Technique:** Ask yourself probing questions to uncover your true internal state. Questions might include, "What beliefs are shaping my current reality?" or "How do my feelings align with the outcomes I desire?" This process can reveal subconscious blocks or patterns that need addressing.

2. **Visualization Techniques:**

   - **Future Self Visualization:** Engage in visualization exercises where you picture your ideal future self living the desired external reality. Focus on the emotions and thoughts this future self embodies, and begin to integrate these into your current state.

- **Daily Visualization Practice:** Make visualization a daily practice, spending a few minutes each day imagining your goals as already achieved. Feel the emotions associated with these achievements to align your internal energy with these outcomes.

3. Affirmative Practice:

- **Create Personal Affirmations:** Craft affirmations that resonate with your desired external outcomes and reflect the internal state needed to achieve them. Repeat these affirmations daily, ideally in the morning and before bed, to embed them into your subconscious.

- **Affirmation Integration:** Integrate your affirmations into your daily life by posting them in visible places, using them as reminders on your phone, or reciting them during challenging moments.

4. Emotional Alignment:

- **Emotional Inventory:** Regularly take an "emotional inventory" to assess your feelings. Acknowledge any emotions that might be out of alignment with your desired outcomes and explore their origins.

- **Emotional Regulation Techniques:** Practice emotional regulation techniques such as deep breathing, mindfulness meditation, or emotional freedom techniques (EFT) to manage and align your emotions with your aspirations.

5. Cultivate a Growth Mindset:

- **Embrace Learning:** View challenges and setbacks as opportunities for learning and growth. This perspective helps maintain a positive internal state, even in the face of adversity.

- **Celebrate Small Wins:** Recognize and celebrate progress towards your goals, no matter how small. This practice fosters a mindset of achievement and possibility.

6. Mindful Consumption:

- **Curate Input:** Be mindful of the information, media, and conversations you engage with. Ensure they are supportive of your desired internal state and external outcomes.

- **Positive Influences:** Surround yourself with positive influences—people, books, podcasts—that align with your goals and inspire you to maintain a constructive internal state.

By incorporating these methods into your personal development routine, you can ensure your internal world—comprising your thoughts, emotions, and beliefs—is optimally aligned with the external outcomes you wish to manifest. This alignment is crucial for harnessing the Law of Correspondence effectively, enabling you to create a reality that reflects your highest aspirations and truest self.

The Principle of Universal Connection

The Principle of Universal Connection illuminates the profound truth that everything in the universe is interconnected. This timeless wisdom, echoed in spiritual traditions and modern science alike, suggests that no element of the cosmos exists in isolation; every particle, every being, every thought, and every action is part of an intricate web of existence. This interconnectedness implies that our actions and states of being have ripples that extend far beyond our immediate perception, influencing the world around us and, in turn, being influenced by it.

The Web of Existence:

Just as a single thread can affect the integrity of an entire web, so too can an individual action influence the larger aspect of life. This principle encourages us to view ourselves not as isolated entities but as integral components of a greater whole. It invites a sense of responsibility towards the well-being of our planet and its inhabitants, recognizing that our individual and collective well-being are deeply intertwined.

The Ripple Effect of Actions:

Every action we take sends out ripples into the universe, affecting others and the environment in ways seen and unseen. Positive actions, no matter how small, contribute to the collective energy of the world, fostering kindness, compassion, and healing. Conversely, negative actions can propagate disharmony and suffering. Understanding this ripple effect motivates us to act with mindfulness and intention, choosing actions that contribute positively to the universal web.

Practical Applications of the Principle of Universal Connection:

1. Mindful Living:

○ Cultivate mindfulness in your daily life, recognizing that your thoughts, words, and actions are interconnected with the greater whole. Make choices that reflect a respect for this interconnectedness.

2. **Environmental Stewardship:**

○ Engage in practices that honor and protect the environment. This can range from reducing waste, supporting sustainable practices, to participating in conservation efforts. Recognizing our connection to the earth encourages stewardship that benefits all beings.

3. **Compassionate Interactions:**

○ Approach interactions with others with compassion and empathy, understanding that we are all connected. Small acts of kindness and understanding can have far-reaching effects, promoting a sense of unity and mutual support.

4. **Community Engagement:**

○ Participate in community activities or initiatives that aim to uplift and support others. Working towards the common good reinforces the principle of universal connection and its positive impact on collective well-being.

5. **Spiritual Practices:**

○ Engage in spiritual or meditative practices that help you feel connected to something greater than yourself. Whether through meditation, prayer, or contemplation, these practices can deepen your sense of interconnectedness.

6. **Learning and Sharing Knowledge:**

   - Seek to learn about cultures, traditions, and perspectives different from your own. Sharing this knowledge can foster understanding and connection across diverse communities, highlighting our shared humanity.

7. **Reflective Journalling:**

   - Regularly reflect on the ways in which you feel connected to others and the world around you. Journalling about these experiences can enhance your awareness of the intricate web of connections that make up your life.

Living mindfully with an awareness of the broader impact of our actions is essential for fostering a harmonious existence within the interconnected web of life. Here are strategies designed to encourage mindful living that respects and enhances our collective well-being:

1. **Conscious Consumption:**
   - **Evaluate Needs vs. Wants:** Before making a purchase, consider whether it is a need or a want. This mindfulness can reduce unnecessary consumption, which impacts resource use and waste production.

   - **Support Sustainable Practices:** Opt for products and services from companies that prioritize sustainability and ethical practices. Your purchasing power can support environmental preservation and fair labor practices.

2. Eco-friendly Lifestyle Choices:

- **Reduce, Reuse, Recycle:** Adopt the principles of reducing waste, reusing items, and recycling materials to minimize your ecological footprint.

- **Energy Conservation:** Be mindful of your energy use by implementing energy-saving measures in your home and daily life, such as using energy-efficient appliances, reducing water usage, and turning off lights when not in use.

3. Mindful Eating:

- **Plant-based Choices:** Incorporate more plant-based foods into your diet. This shift can significantly lower your carbon footprint and promote animal welfare.

- **Local and Seasonal Foods:** Whenever possible, choose local and seasonal foods. This supports local farmers, reduces transportation emissions, and ensures fresher, more nutritious meals.

4. Compassionate Communication:

- **Active Listening:** Practice active listening in conversations, giving your full attention to the speaker. This fosters deeper connections and understanding.

- **Thoughtful Responses:** Consider the impact of your words before speaking. Aim to communicate in ways that are kind, constructive, and respectful of others' perspectives.

5. Community Involvement:

- **Volunteer Your Time:** Engage in volunteer work that contributes to the well-being of your community or the environment. This can range from participating in local clean-up efforts to helping at a food bank.

- **Advocate for Positive Change:** Use your voice to advocate for policies and initiatives that promote sustainability, equality, and compassion in your community and beyond.

6. Personal Growth and Development:

- **Continuous Learning:** Stay informed about global issues and the impact of individual and collective actions. Seek knowledge that empowers you to live more sustainably and compassionately.

- **Self-Reflection:** Regularly reflect on your actions, attitudes, and their impacts. Consider how you can align more closely with the values of mindfulness and interconnectedness.

7. Mindful Technology Use:

- **Digital Detox:** Regularly take breaks from digital devices to reconnect with yourself, others, and nature. This can help reduce the environmental impact of digital consumption and improve your mental well-being.

- **Purposeful Online Engagement:** Be intentional about your use of social media and digital platforms. Share and engage with content that promotes positive messages, mindfulness, and awareness of interconnectedness.

8. Financial Contributions:

- **Support Causes You Believe In:** Donate to organizations and causes that work towards environmental conservation, social justice, and other efforts that aim to improve the collective well-being.

- **Ethical Investing:** Consider the impact of your investments. Support businesses and projects that are committed to ethical, sustainable, and socially responsible practices.

Enhancing awareness of one's role in the universal web of interconnectedness is fundamental to living a life that acknowledges and nurtures the connections between our actions and the broader cosmos. Here are practices designed to deepen your understanding and appreciation of this intricate relationship:

1. Nature Immersion:

- **Regular Nature Walks:** Spend time in nature regularly, whether it's a walk in the park, a hike in the forest, or simply sitting by a body of water. Use this time to observe the natural world and reflect on your place within it.

- **Nature Meditation:** Practice meditation in natural settings. Focus on the sounds, smells, and sensations of the environment around you. This can help foster a deep sense of connection with the earth and all its inhabitants.

2. Ecological Footprint Awareness:

- **Calculate Your Footprint:** Use online tools to calculate your ecological footprint. Understanding the impact of your lifestyle on the planet can be an eye-opening experience that motivates more sustainable living practices.

- **Sustainable Living Changes:** Based on your footprint analysis, make conscious changes to reduce your impact.

This could involve altering your diet, transportation habits, consumption patterns, or energy usage.

3. Mindful Consumption:

- **Intentional Purchasing:** Before buying anything, ask yourself if it's necessary, how it was produced, and what its environmental and social impact might be. Opt for products that are ethical, sustainable, and contribute positively to the community.

- **Minimalist Lifestyle:** Explore minimalism as a way to reduce consumption and live more intentionally. Focusing on what truly adds value to your life can decrease the demand for resources and reduce waste.

4. Journaling for Connection:

- **Reflective Journaling:** Regularly journal about your experiences, thoughts, and feelings regarding your connection to the universal web. Reflect on how your actions impact the world around you and how external changes affect your inner state.

- **Gratitude Journaling:** Incorporate gratitude for the natural world and its resources into your daily journaling practice. Acknowledging the gifts of nature can enhance your sense of responsibility towards preserving them.

5. Community Engagement:

- **Participate in Community Projects:** Get involved in local environmental or social projects that aim to improve your community. Working with others towards a common goal can reinforce your sense of interconnectedness.

- **Create or Join a Sharing Economy:** Engage in or establish community sharing initiatives, like tool libraries, community gardens, or car-sharing programs. These efforts can reduce consumption and foster a sense of community.

6. Educate and Advocate:

- **Self-Education:** Commit to ongoing education about environmental issues, social justice, and sustainability. Understanding these topics can deepen your awareness of your role in the universal web.

- **Advocacy:** Use your voice to advocate for policies and practices that protect the environment and promote social equity. Advocacy can be a powerful tool for change, influencing others and amplifying your impact.

7. Spiritual Practices:

- **Connective Meditation and Prayer:** Engage in meditation or prayer practices that focus on the connection between all forms of life. Such practices can foster a sense of unity and compassion.

- **Study Interconnectedness Philosophies:** Explore philosophies and spiritual teachings that emphasize the interconnectedness of all things, such as Buddhism, Indigenous wisdom, or systems theory. These teachings can offer valuable insights into your role within the universal web.

8. Creative Expression:

- **Artistic Projects:** Use art, writing, music, or other forms of creative expression to explore and communicate your understanding of interconnectedness. Creative projects can be a powerful means of reflecting on and sharing your insights.

By integrating these practices into your life, you not only enhance your awareness of your interconnected role within the cosmos but also actively contribute to the well-being of the planet and all its inhabitants. Living with this consciousness can transform your actions into expressions of care and reverence for the intricate web of life, fostering a more sustainable, compassionate, and connected world.

Chapter Thirteen

The Law of Gender

This principle is not about gender in a biological or social context but rather about the energetic qualities traditionally ascribed to masculine and feminine principles. Understanding and harmonizing these energies within ourselves and in our interactions with the world can lead to greater equilibrium, creativity, and well-being.

Masculine and Feminine Energies Explained:

- **Masculine Energy:** Often associated with qualities such as logic, action, decisiveness, and strength. It is the force that initiates, protects, and provides structure.

- **Feminine Energy:** Traditionally linked with intuition, nurturing, receptivity, and creativity. It embodies the capacity to flow, adapt, and nurture growth and healing.

Both energies are present to varying degrees in everyone, regardless of gender, and learning to recognize, balance, and harness these energies is key to personal and spiritual development.

Balancing Masculine and Feminine Energies:
1. **Self-Reflection:**

   - Regularly assess your own balance of masculine and feminine energies. Reflect on which qualities you naturally embody and which may need more expression or development.

2. **Mindful Integration:**

   - Intentionally incorporate practices that cultivate the energy you wish to develop more fully. For example, if you wish to enhance your feminine energy, you might engage in more creative activities or practice listening to your intuition. Conversely, to boost masculine energy, you might focus on setting and achieving goals or developing assertiveness.

3. Meditation and Visualization:

- Use meditation and visualization techniques to harmonize your masculine and feminine energies. Visualize these energies flowing and balancing within you, each supporting and enhancing the other.

4. Healing Work:

- Engage in healing practices to address and resolve any wounds or blockages related to your masculine or feminine aspects. This may involve therapy, energy healing, or self-care practices that nurture your whole self.

5. Relationship Reflection:

- Consider how your balance of energies influences your relationships. Are there patterns that might be attributed to an imbalance? Reflect on ways to bring more harmony into your interactions with others.

Applying the Law of Gender in Daily Life:

1. Creative Expression:

- Use art, music, writing, or dance as a means to explore and express the interplay of masculine and feminine energies within you. Creative endeavors can be a powerful avenue for bringing these energies into balance.

2. Conscious Communication:

- Practice communicating in a way that honors both assertiveness and empathy, allowing you to express your needs and boundaries while remaining open and receptive to the needs of others.

3. Holistic Decision-Making:

- Make decisions that consider both logical analysis and intuitive guidance. This approach ensures a balanced consideration of practical and emotional aspects.

4. Collaborative Endeavors:

- Engage in projects or activities that require a balance of action and receptivity, planning and adaptability, demonstrating the strength of combining masculine and feminine energies.

5. Spiritual Practices:

- Incorporate spiritual or religious practices that honor the divine masculine and feminine. Many traditions celebrate these energies through deities, rituals, or teachings that can offer deeper insights into their balance and integration.

Harmonizing masculine and feminine energies within oneself is a journey of self-discovery, acceptance, and integration. By achieving this balance, you can tap into a more profound sense of wholeness and well-being. Here are tips to help you harmonize these energies:

1. Awareness and Acknowledgment:

- Begin by becoming aware of the masculine and feminine aspects within you. Acknowledge that everyone possesses a unique blend of these energies, regardless of gender. Reflect on how these energies manifest in your thoughts, emotions, and behaviors.

2. Cultivate the Underrepresented Energy:

- Identify which energy is less dominant or underrepresented in your life. Engage in activities that cultivate this energy. For instance, if you need to balance with more feminine energy, you might explore activities that foster creativity, intuition, and emotional expression. Conversely, if you seek more masculine energy, consider activities that build confidence, assertiveness, and goal orientation.

3. Mindful Meditation and Visualization:

- Practice meditation that focuses on balancing masculine and feminine energies. Visualize these energies harmonizing within your body, perhaps as complementary colors or symbols that merge and balance each other out.

4. Integrate Both Energies in Decision-Making:

- Make conscious decisions that incorporate both logical (masculine) and intuitive (feminine) inputs. Before making a decision, consider the facts and practical aspects while also listening to your gut feelings and emotional responses.

5. Practice Emotional Fluidity:

- Allow yourself to experience and express a full range of emotions, from strength and assertiveness to vulnerability and empathy. Recognizing that all emotions are valid and can be expressed healthily is key to balancing masculine and feminine energies.

6. Engage in Physical Activities that Foster Balance:

- Certain physical practices like yoga, tai chi, or dance emphasize balance, fluidity, and strength, helping to harmonize masculine and feminine energies within the body.

7. Creative Expression:

- Use creative outlets such as writing, painting, music, or other art forms to explore and express the interplay of your masculine and feminine energies. Creative activities can be powerful tools for uncovering and integrating these aspects of yourself.

8. Foster Relationships that Encourage Balance:

- Cultivate relationships that support and reflect a healthy balance of masculine and feminine energies. Surround yourself with people who embody traits you wish to develop and who encourage you to express your whole self.

9. Reflect on Role Models:

- Identify and reflect on role models or figures in your life (or from history, literature, etc.) who embody a balanced integration of masculine and feminine energies. Consider the qualities they possess and how you might incorporate similar attributes into your own life.

10. Rituals and Practices for Balance:

- Create personal rituals that honor both the masculine and feminine within you. This might include writing affirmations that affirm both sets of qualities, or it could involve rituals that symbolize the union of these energies, such as combining elements (water and fire, earth and air) in a meaningful way.

Balancing and exploring personal expressions of masculine and feminine energies can enhance your life in numerous ways, fostering a sense of completeness and harmony. Here are activities specifically designed to help you explore and balance these energies within yourself:

1. Role Reversal Experimentation:

- If you find yourself predominantly expressing one energy, consciously adopt roles or tasks that require the opposite energy. For example, if you're typically action-oriented (masculine), try engaging in more nurturing, receptive activities (feminine), such as cooking for loved ones or practicing active listening.

2. Creative Arts Exploration:

- Use art to express and explore your masculine and feminine energies. Draw, paint, or create two pieces: one that represents your masculine side and another for your feminine side. This can provide visual insight into the balance or dominance of these energies within you.

3. Movement and Dance:

- Participate in dance or movement practices that encourage the expression of both energies. For example, martial arts can help cultivate focus and assertiveness (masculine), while fluid dance forms like contemporary dance can enhance intuition and grace (feminine).

4. Guided Imagery Meditation:

- Practice guided meditations that focus on balancing masculine and feminine energies. Visualize a place where these energies manifest in nature (e.g., a mountain and a river) and see them working together in harmony, reflecting the balance you wish to achieve within yourself.

5. Affirmation Creation:

- Write affirmations that honor both your masculine and feminine aspects. For example, "I am strong and assertive, yet compassionate and receptive." Recite these affirmations daily to reinforce the balance of energies.

6. Explore Archetypes:

- Research and reflect on various archetypes that embody masculine and feminine qualities (e.g., the warrior, the nurturer). Journal about how these archetypes resonate with you and how you might embody their balanced qualities in your life.

7. Energy Healing Practices:

- Engage in energy healing practices, such as Reiki or Qi Gong, that focus on harmonizing the body's energies. These practices can help clear blockages and promote a balanced flow of masculine and feminine energies.

8. Nature Connection Activities:

- Spend time in nature observing the balance of masculine and feminine qualities around you (e.g., the strength of trees and the nurturing quality of water). Reflect on how these qualities manifest in harmony and consider how you might replicate this balance in your own life.

9. Masculine and Feminine Energy Days:
- Designate days where you focus on expressing and cultivating one energy at a time. For instance, dedicate one day to activities that highlight your masculine energy and another day to those that enhance your feminine energy. This can help you appreciate and develop each aspect of yourself more fully.

By engaging in these activities, you can gain a deeper understanding and appreciation of the masculine and feminine energies within you. Balancing these energies leads to a more holistic self-expression and a fulfilling life, enriched by the dynamic interplay of strength and receptivity, action and reflection.

Chapter Fourteen

Conclusion

Each law, distinct in its nature, contributes to the entirety of existence, guiding us towards a deeper understanding of the universe and our place within it. Together, they form a symphony of wisdom that, when understood and applied, can lead to a life of greater harmony, purpose, and fulfillment.

1. **The Law of Divine Oneness:** Reminds us that everything is connected to everything else. What we think, say, do, and believe will have a corresponding effect on others and the universe around us.

2. **The Law of Vibration:** Asserts that everything in the universe moves and vibrates at its own frequency. By changing our frequency, we can change our reality.

3. **The Law of Correspondence:** Demonstrates that the principles or laws of physics that explain the physical world - energy, Light, vibration, and motion - have their corresponding principles in the etheric or universe. "As above, so below."

4. **The Law of Attraction:** Shows how we create the things,

events, and people that come into our lives. Our thoughts, feelings, words, and actions produce energies which, in turn, attract like energies.

5. **The Law of Inspired Action:** We must take action that supports our thoughts, dreams, emotions, and words.

6. **The Law of Perpetual Transmutation of Energy:** Highlights the ability of everyone to change the conditions in their lives. Higher vibrations consume and transform lower ones; thus, each of us can change the energies in our lives by understanding the Universal Laws and applying the principles in such a way as to effect change.

7. **The Law of Cause and Effect:** Nothing happens by chance or outside the Universal Laws. Every action has a reaction or consequence and we "reap what we have sown."

8. **The Law of Compensation:** Blessings and abundance provided to us for the good deeds we perform and being a reflection of our contributions to humanity.

9. **The Law of Relativity:** Each person will receive a series of problems (Tests of Initiation/Lessons) for the purpose of strengthening the Light within. We must consider each of these tests to be a challenge and remain connected to our hearts when proceeding to solve the problems.

10. **The Law of Polarity:** Everything is on a continuum and has an opposite. We can transform undesirable thoughts by concentrating on the opposite pole. It is the law of mental vibrations.

11. **The Law of Rhythm:** Everything vibrates and moves to certain rhythms. These rhythms establish seasons, cycles, stages of development, and patterns. Each cycle reflects the regularity of God's Universe.

12. **The Law of Gender:** The law that governs what we know as creation. The law of gender manifests in all things as masculine and feminine. It is this law that governs what we know as creation. The word creation is often erroneously used, for, in reality, nothing is ever created. All new things merely result from the changing of something that was, into something else that now is.

As we draw our exploration of the 12 Universal Laws to a close, it's important to remember that understanding these laws is just the beginning of a lifelong journey. The true depth of these principles unfolds through continuous exploration, application, and reflection. Each day offers a new opportunity to witness these laws in action, to learn from our experiences, and to consciously create our reality in harmony with the cosmic order.

Embrace Continuous Learning:
The universe is a vast, ever-expanding classroom filled with lessons on love, growth, resilience, and interconnectedness. Keep an open mind and heart as you delve deeper into the mysteries of these universal laws. Books, workshops, and discussions can provide further insights, but remember, the most profound understanding often comes from personal experience and introspection.

Practice Mindful Application:
Integrating the 12 Universal Laws into your daily life requires mindfulness and intention. Start small by focusing on one law at a time,

observing how it manifests in your life and experimenting with ways to align your actions with its principles. As you become more attuned to the influence of these laws, gradually expand your practice to encompass multiple laws simultaneously, weaving them into the fabric of your daily existence.

Reflect and Journal:

I've repeatedly mentioned how important it is to maintain a journal dedicated to your journey with the Universal Laws. Record your observations, experiences, and insights related to each law. Reflecting on your progress and challenges will not only deepen your understanding but also highlight areas for growth and improvement.

Cultivate Patience and Compassion:

The path to mastering these laws is neither straight nor without obstacles. Practice patience and compassion with yourself as you navigate this journey. Celebrate your successes, learn from your setbacks, and remain compassionate towards yourself and others as you all strive to live in harmony with these timeless principles.

Share Your Journey:

Sharing your experiences with the Universal Laws can be incredibly rewarding. Whether through conversations, social media, blogging, or leading workshops, sharing can deepen your understanding and inspire others to explore these principles. Community and connection are vital aspects of our universal journey.

Live in Gratitude and Wonder:

Approach each day with gratitude and a sense of wonder for the intricate beauty of the universe and its laws. Cultivating a grateful heart opens you to receive the abundance of the universe and to recognize the miraculous ways in which these laws weave through our lives.

Embrace Your Role as a Co-Creator:

Remember, you are a powerful co-creator with the universe. Your thoughts, emotions, and actions have a profound impact on the world around you. By aligning with the Universal Laws, you harness this power to create a life of joy, abundance, and fulfillment, contributing to the greater good of all.

Your Voice Matters:

I encourage you to share your reflections, insights, and experiences with these universal principles. How have they influenced your perspective on life, your interactions with others, and your personal growth? Which laws resonated with you the most, and how have you integrated them into your daily life?

Seeking Your Feedback:

Your feedback is a gift that can illuminate aspects of this journey that are most impactful, areas that may require further exploration, and ways in which this exploration can be made even more relevant and transformative for others.

A Request for Reviews:

If this journey has inspired, challenged, or supported you in any way, I kindly ask that you consider leaving a review. Your reviews not only help others discover this guide but deepen our collective understanding of these timeless principles.

Thank you for being an integral part of this journey. Your engagement, reflection, and willingness to share your experience are what make this exploration so meaningful. May your path forward be illuminated by the light of understanding and the warmth of universal connection.